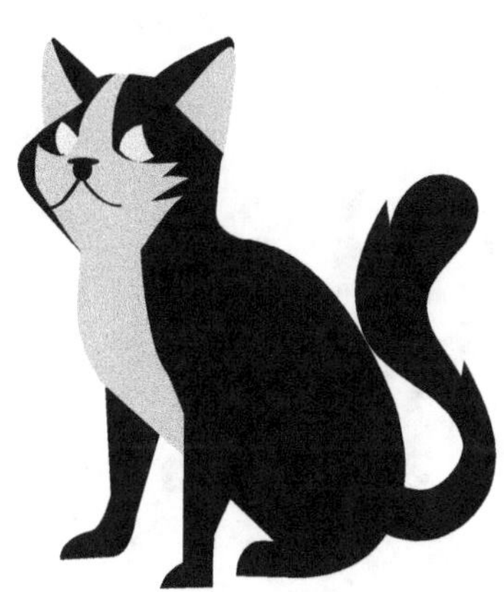

This book belongs to

0 Zero

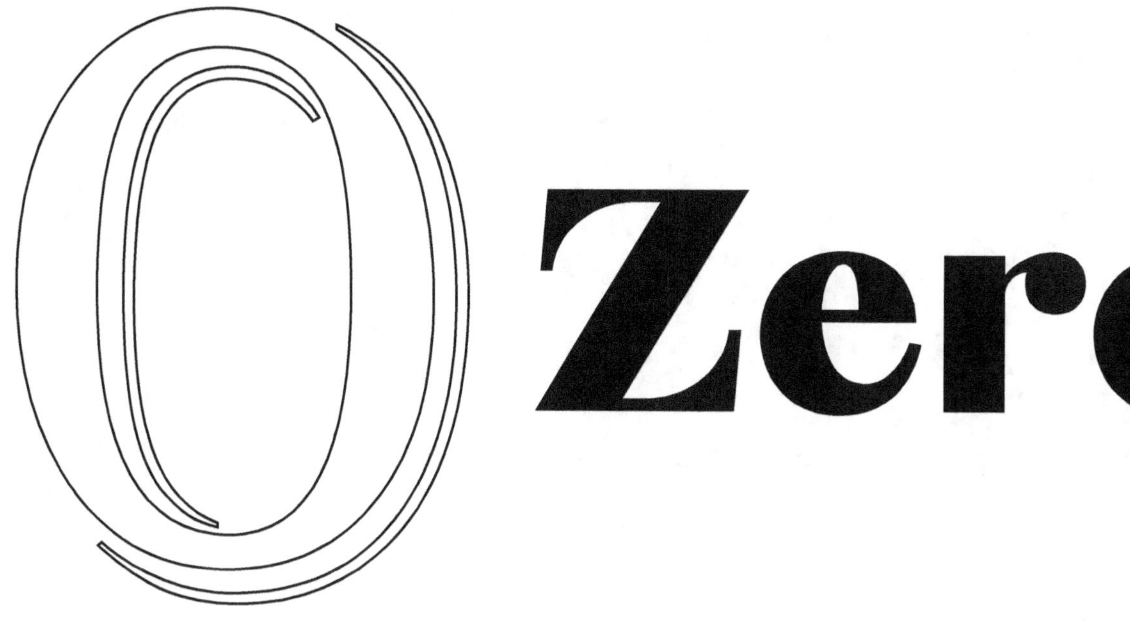

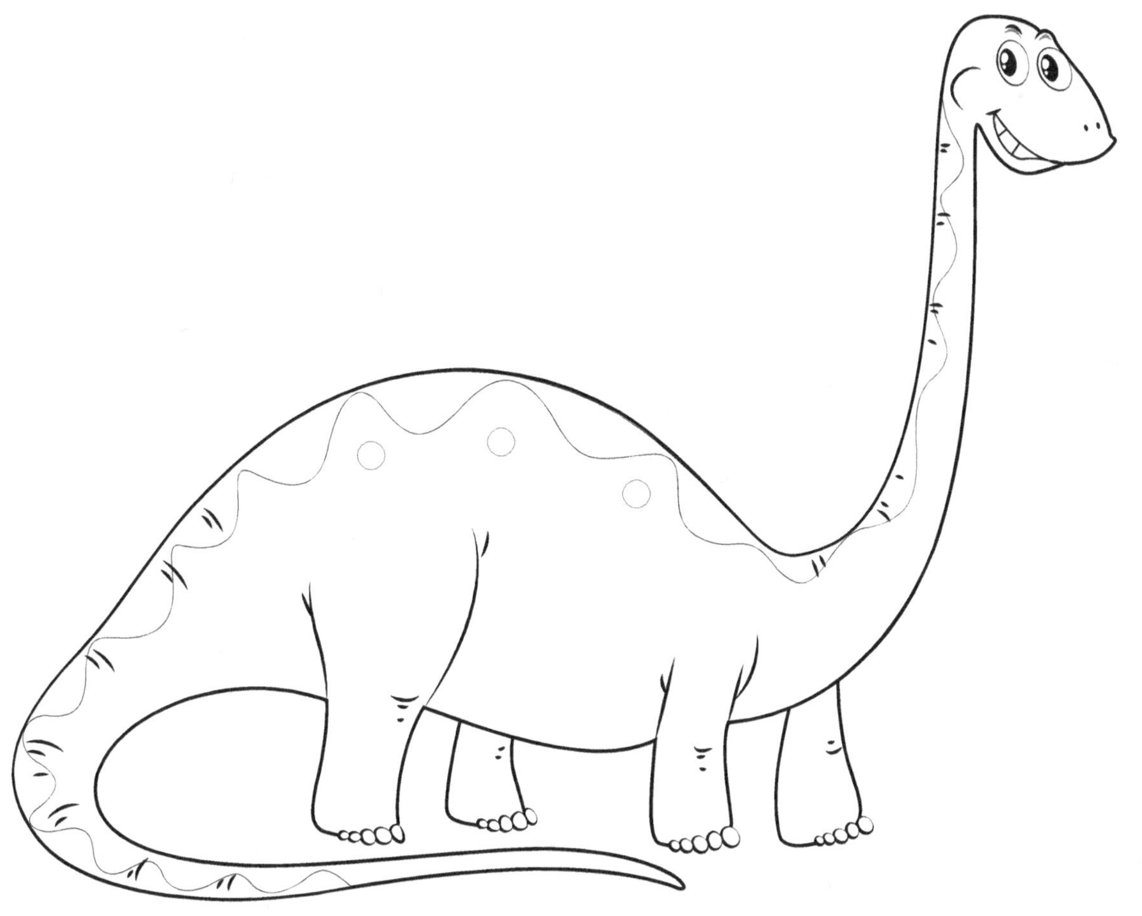

0

Color and Trace

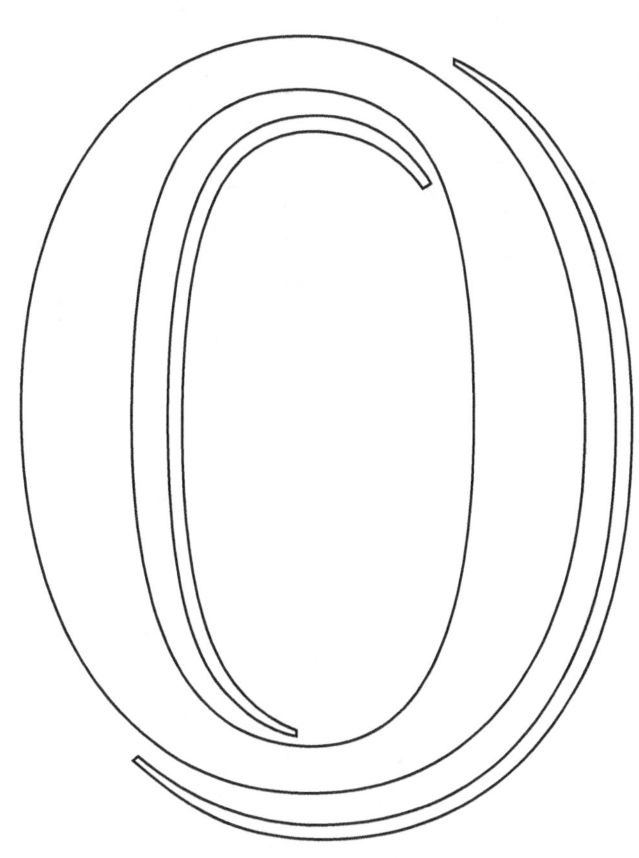

Trace the word ZERO

zero   zero   zero

zero   zero   zero

zero   zero   zero

1 One

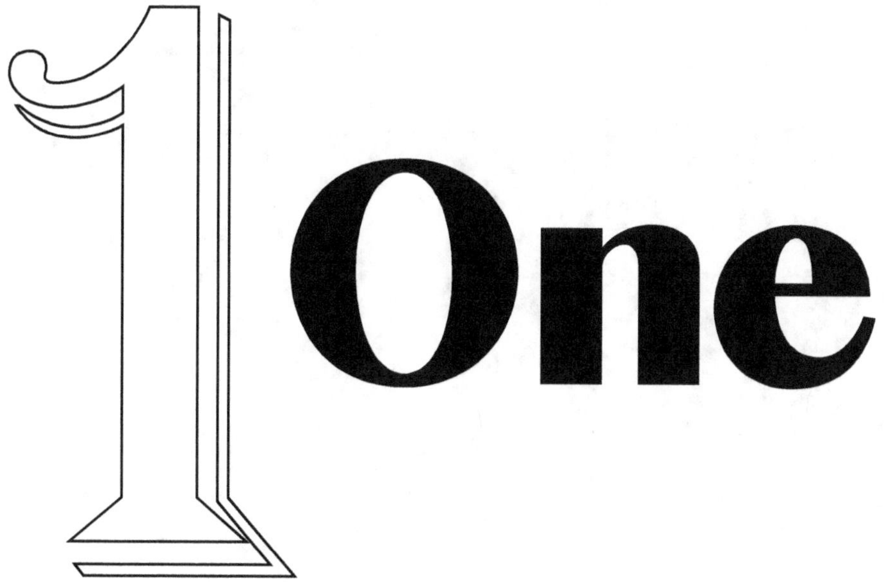

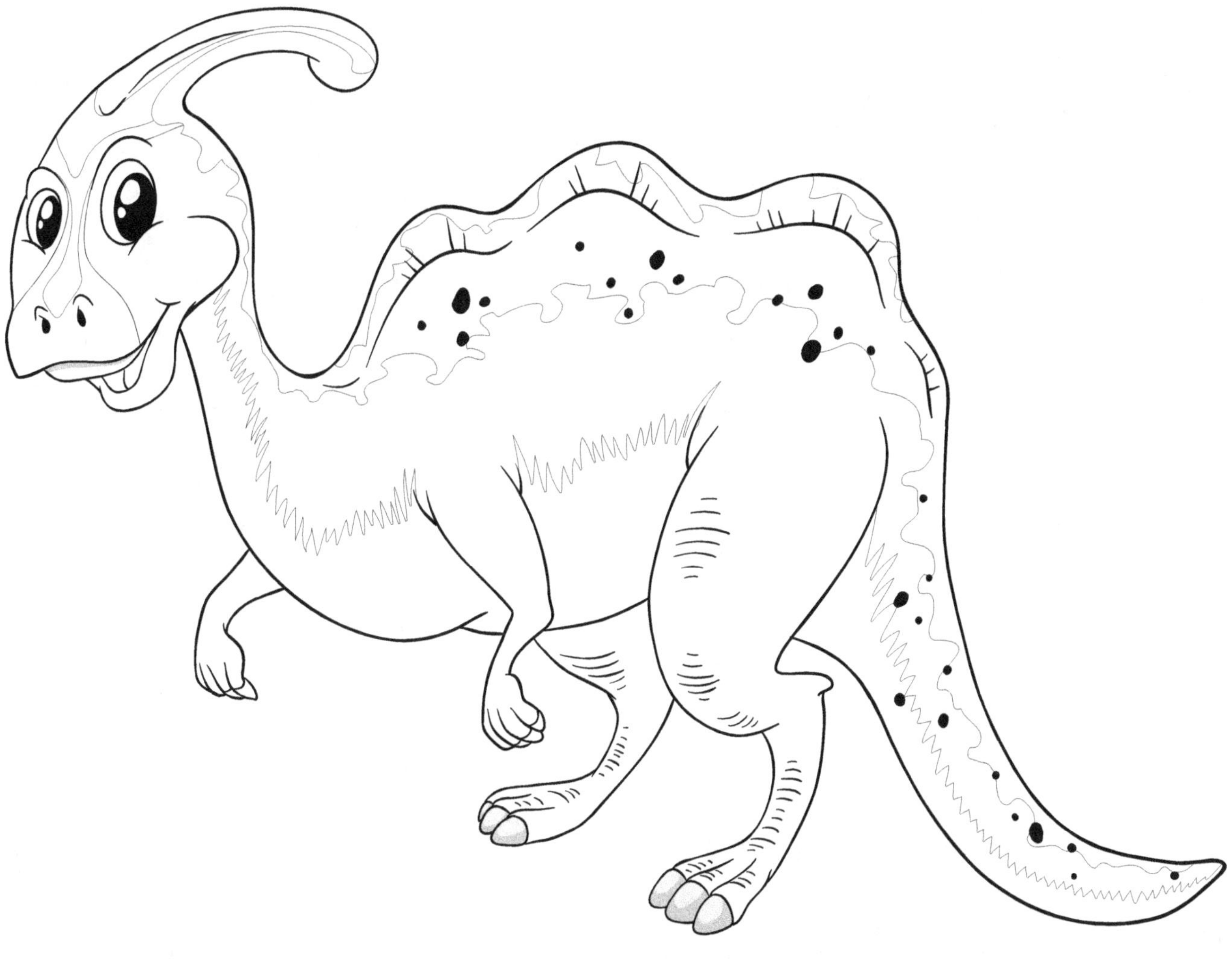

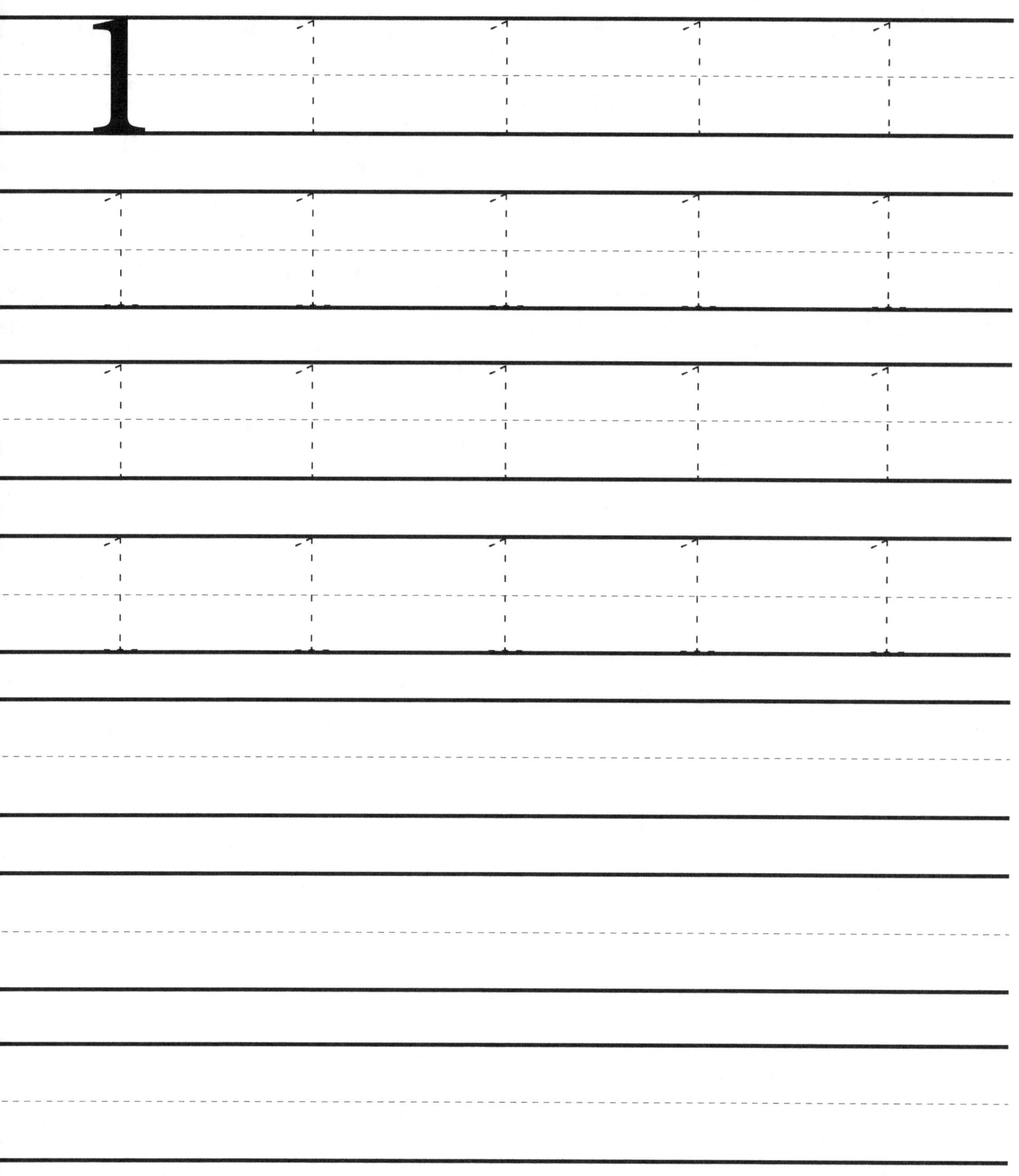

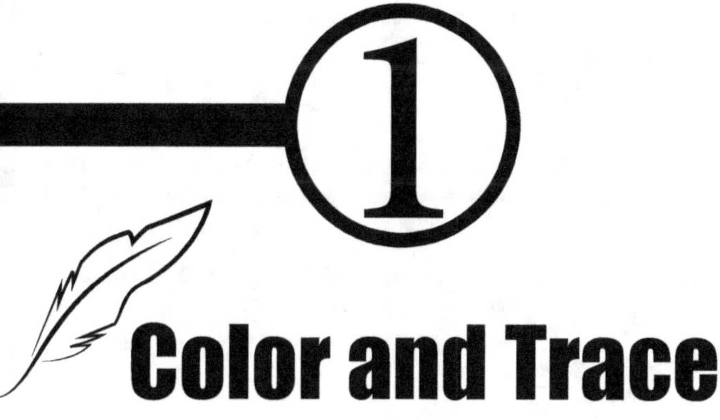

Color and Trace

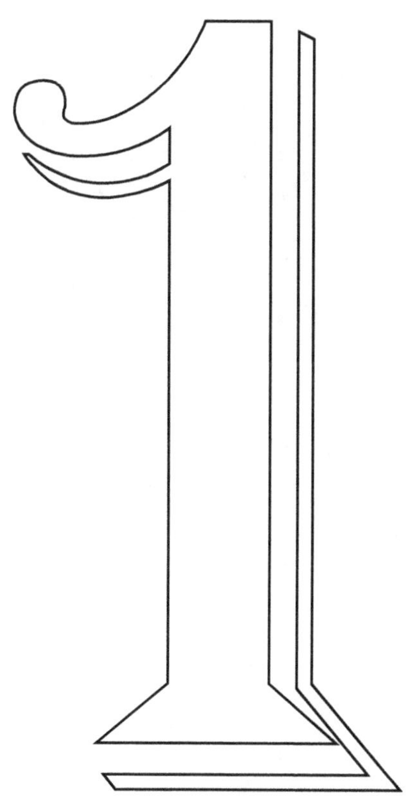

Trace the word ONE

one   one   one

one   one   one

one   one   one

2 Two

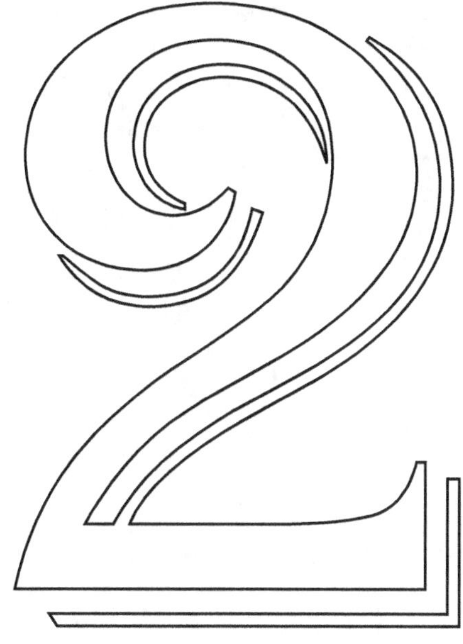

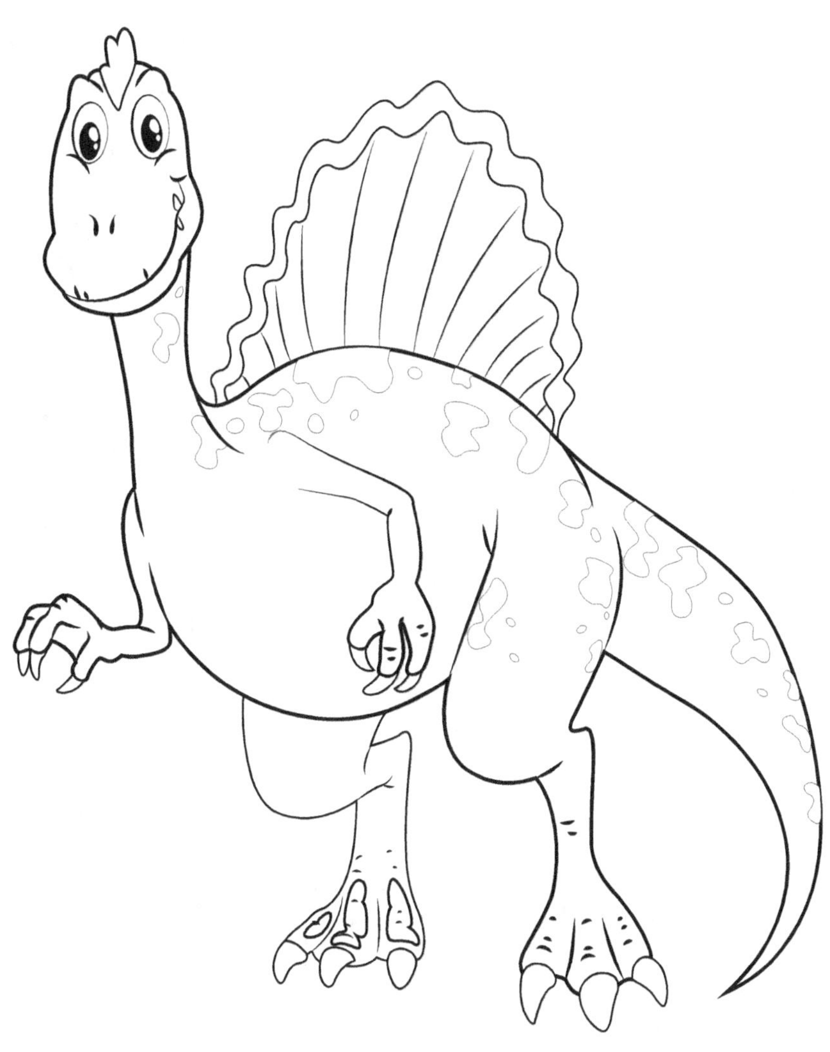

2

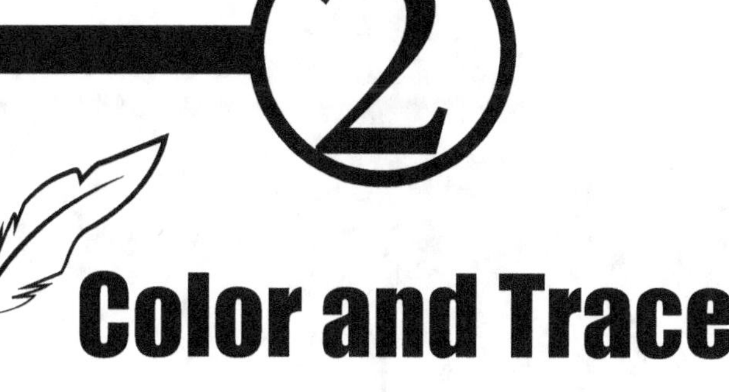

Color and Trace

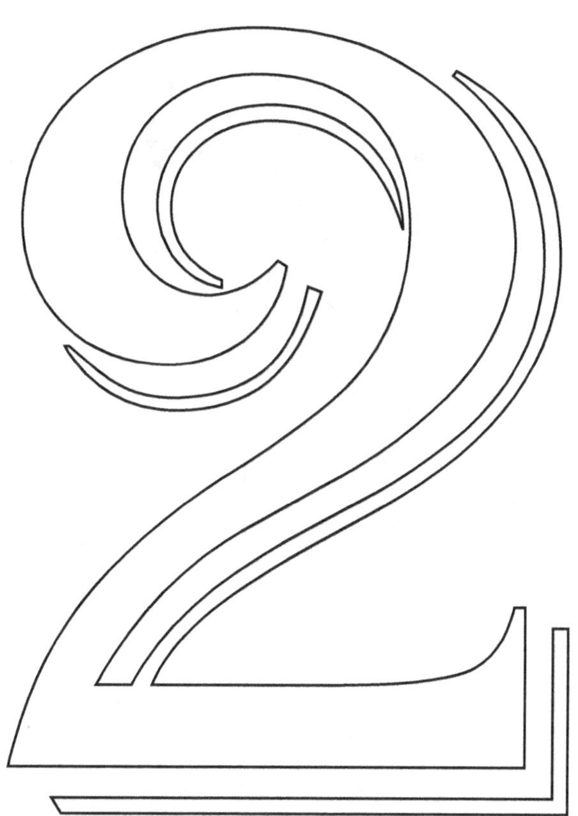

Trace the word TWO

TWO

3 Three

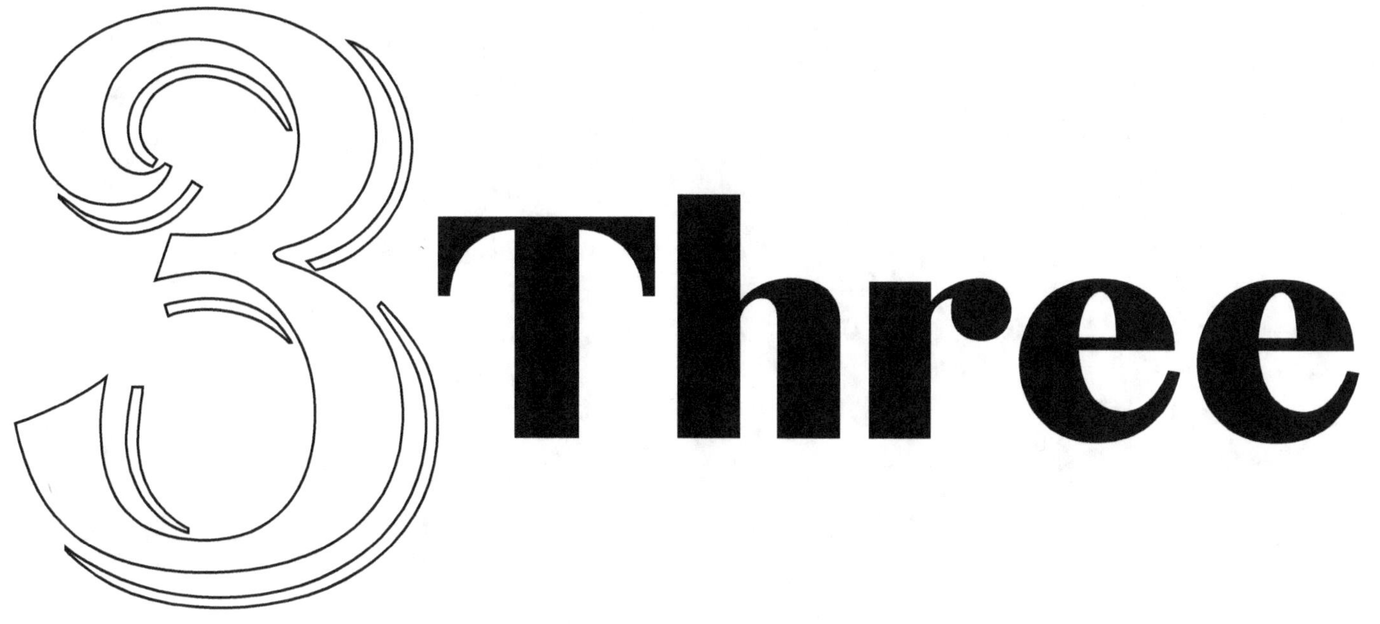

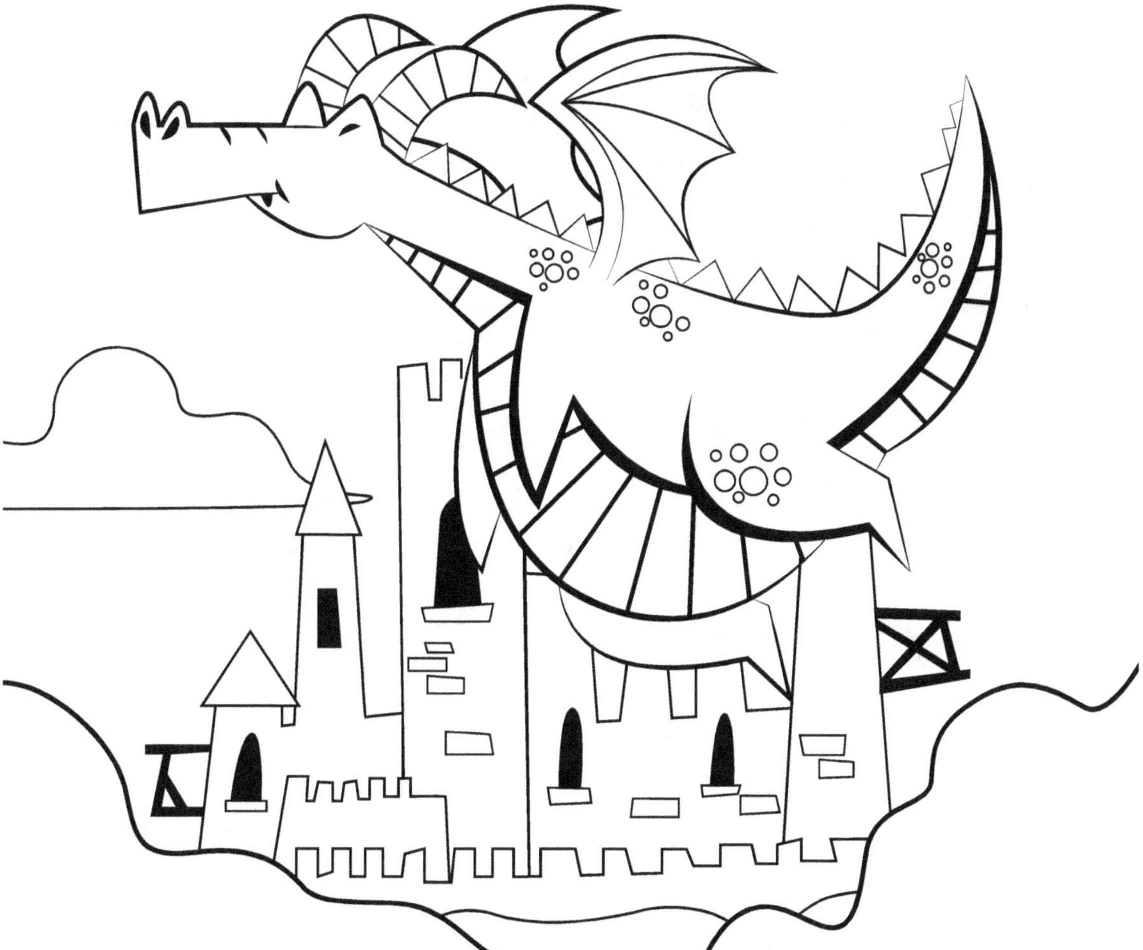

Trace the number

Color and Trace

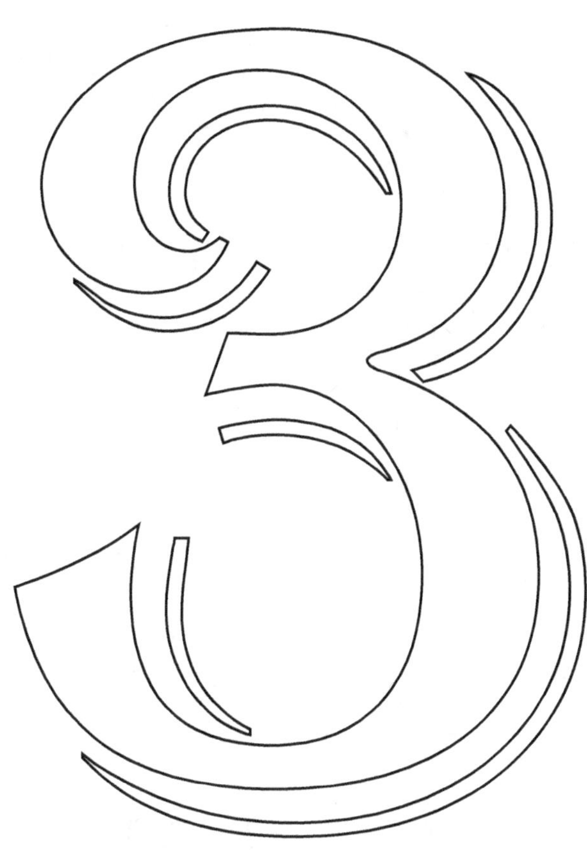

Trace the word THREE

Three   Three   Three

Three   Three   Three

Three   Three   Three

4 Four

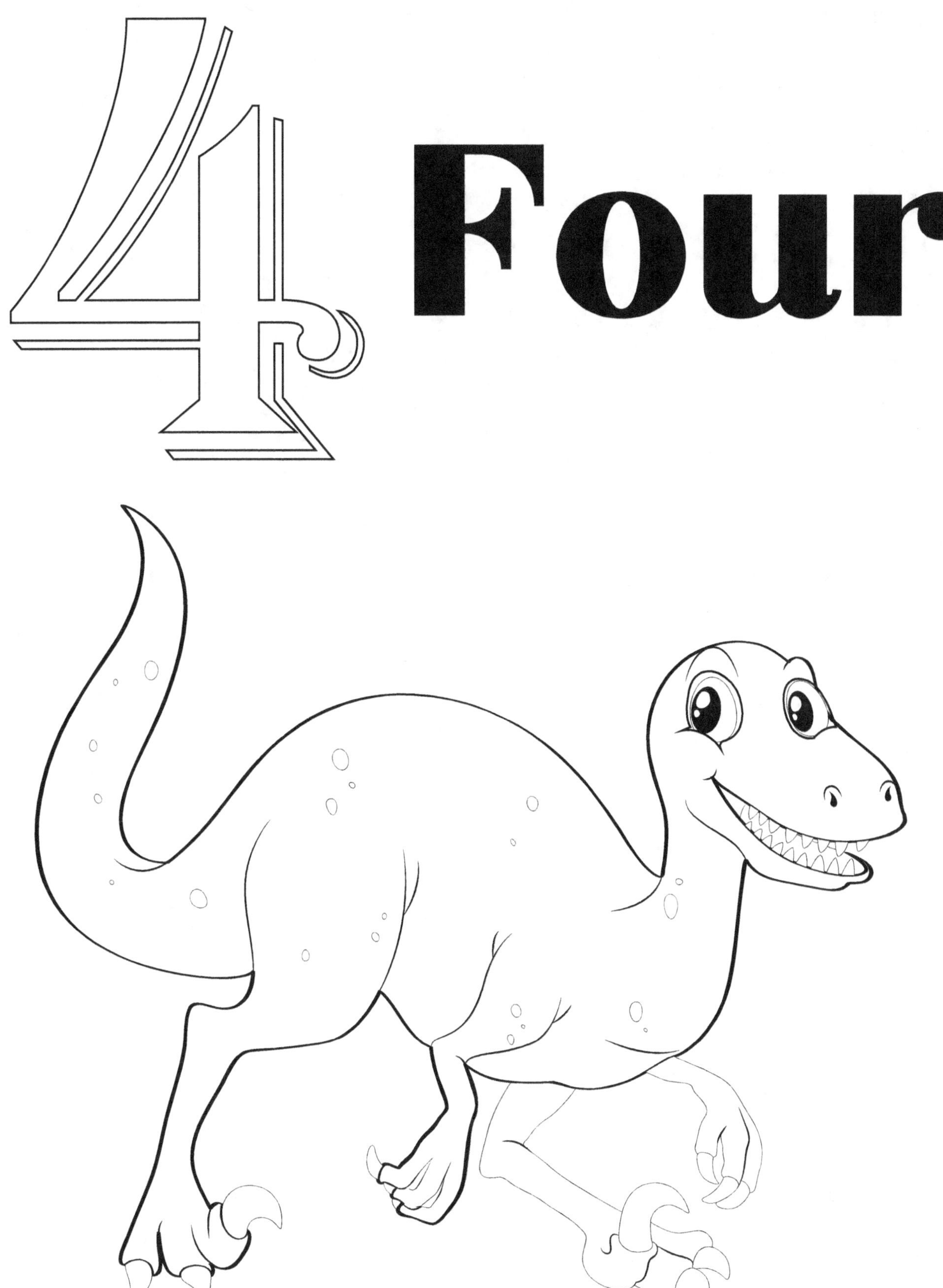

4

Color and Trace

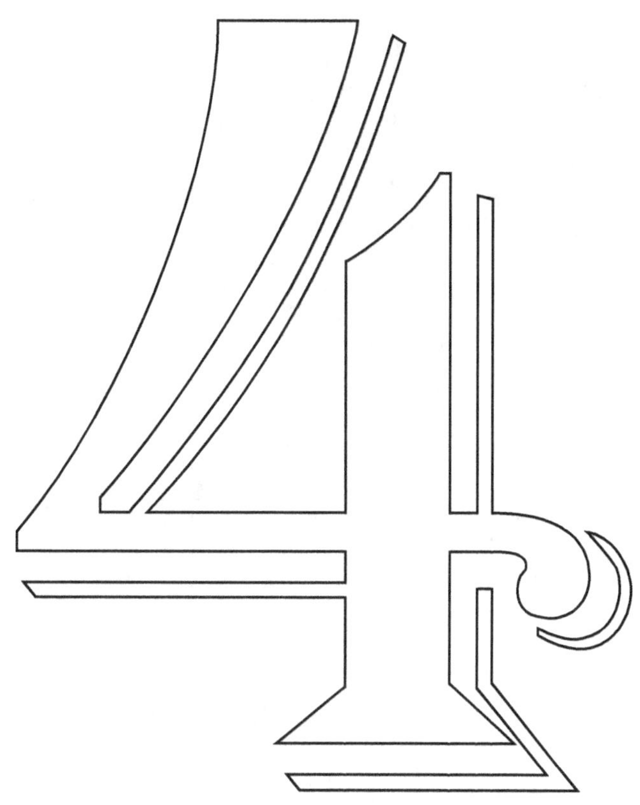

Trace the word FOUR

Four four four

four four four

four four four

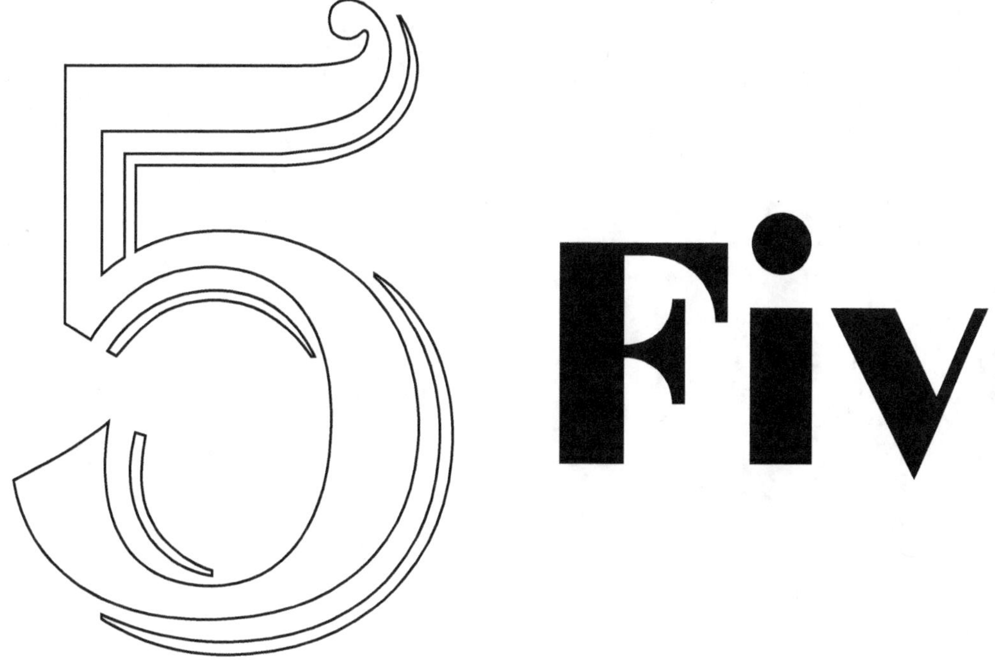

5 Five

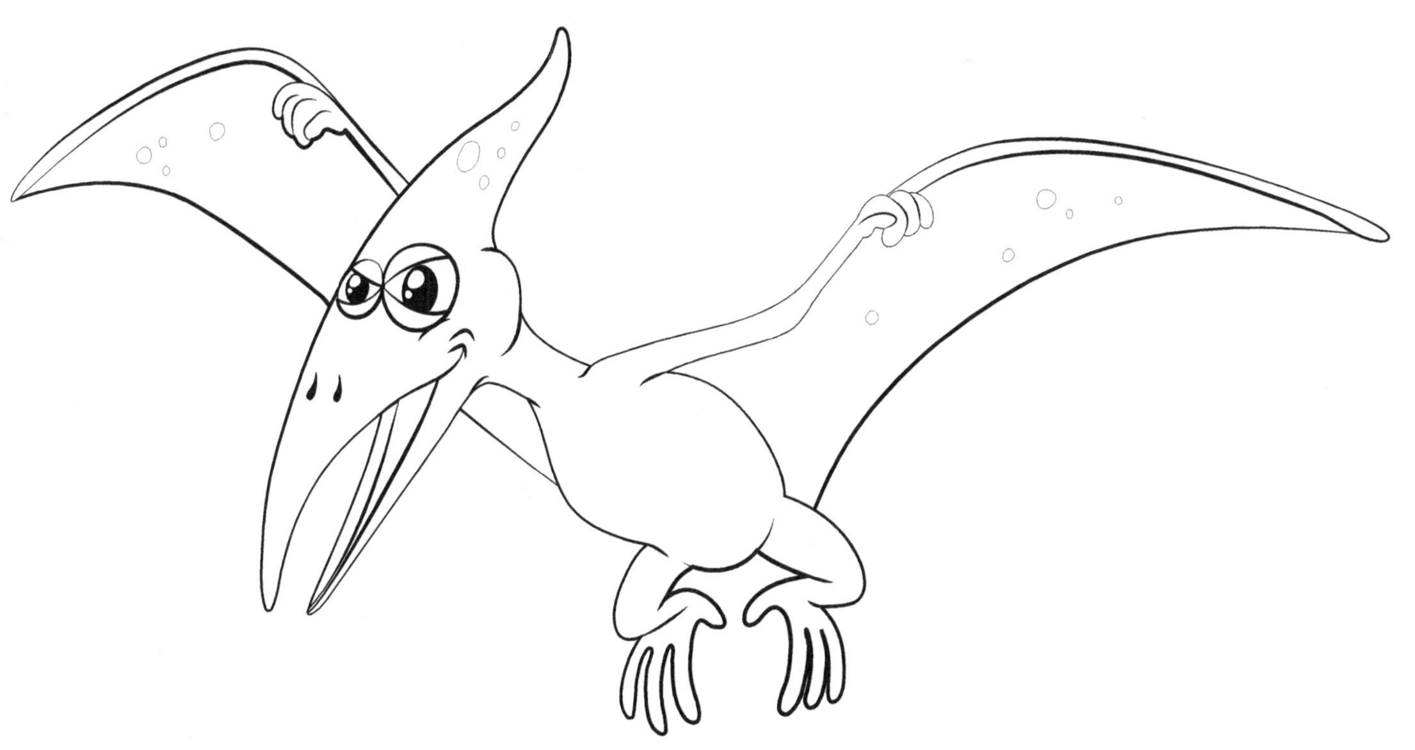

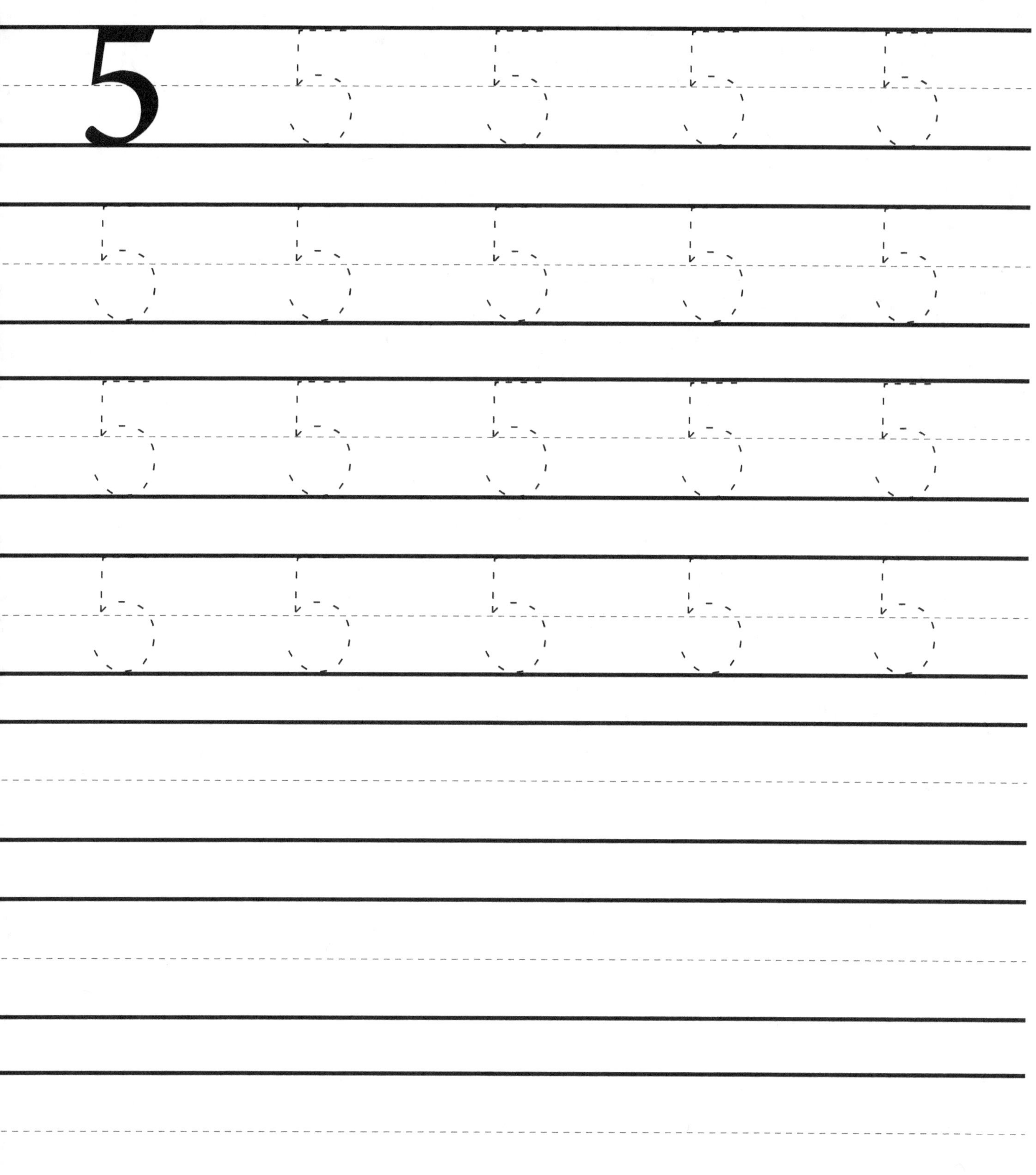

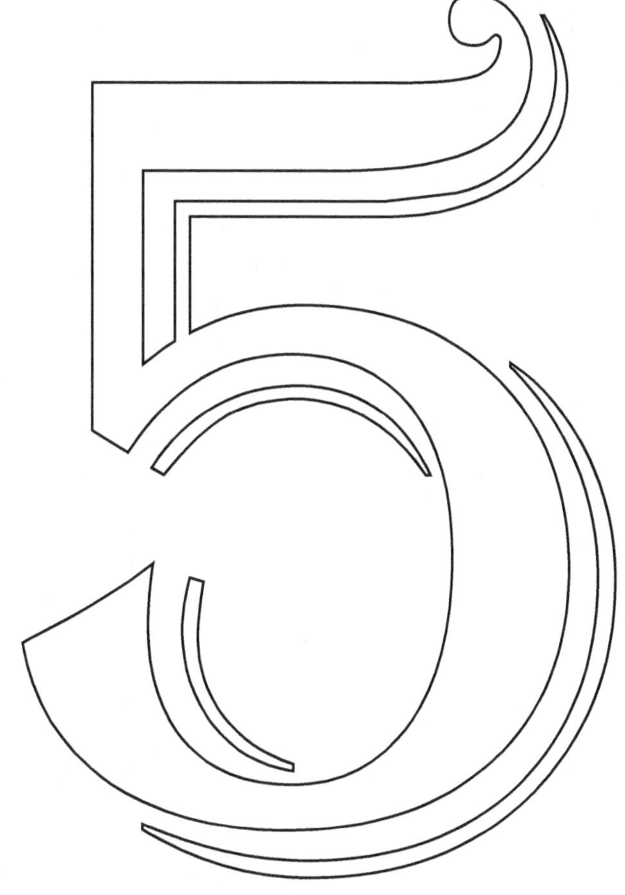

⑤ Color and Trace

Trace the word FIVE

Five

6 Six

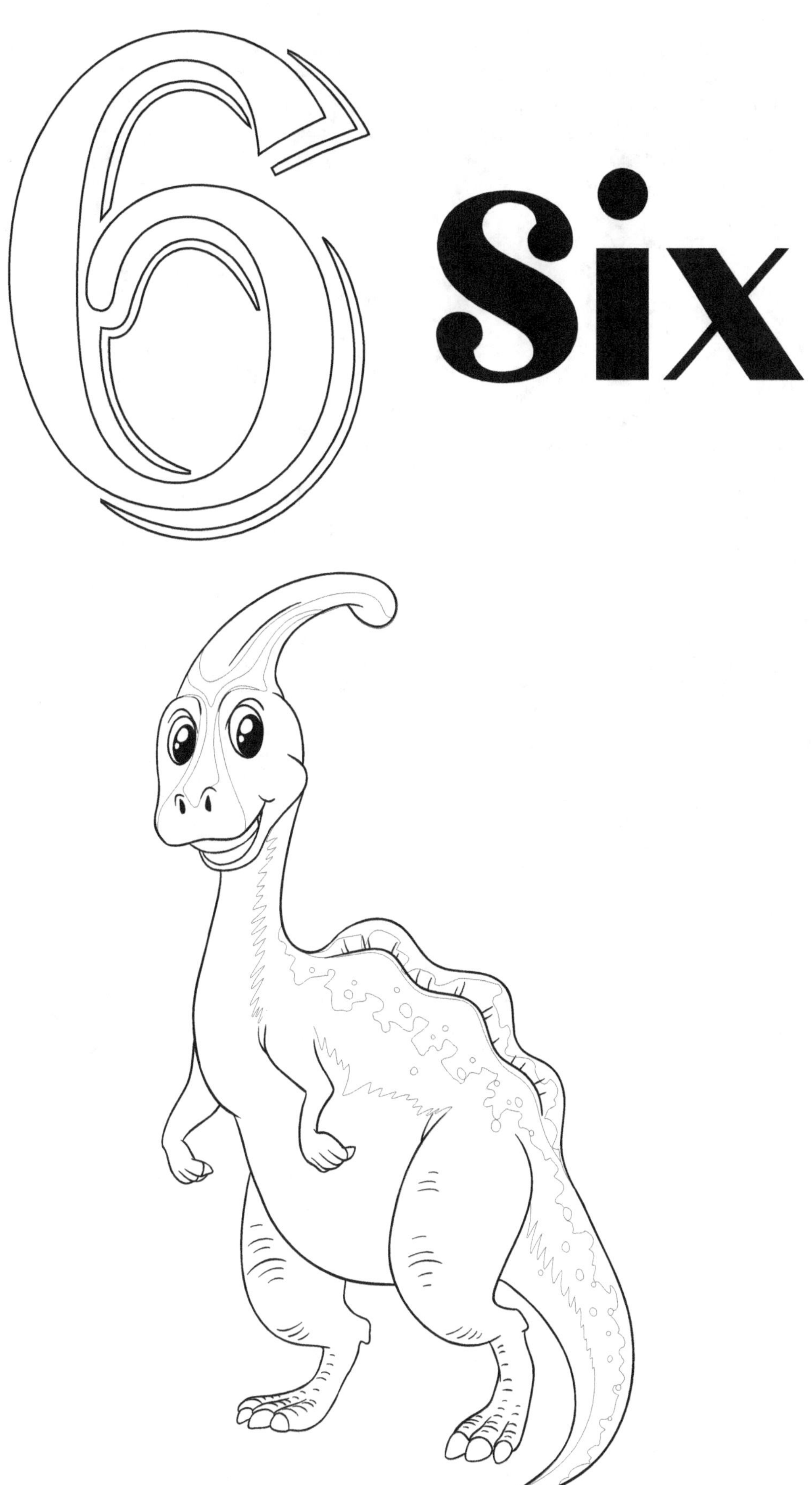

6

Color and Trace

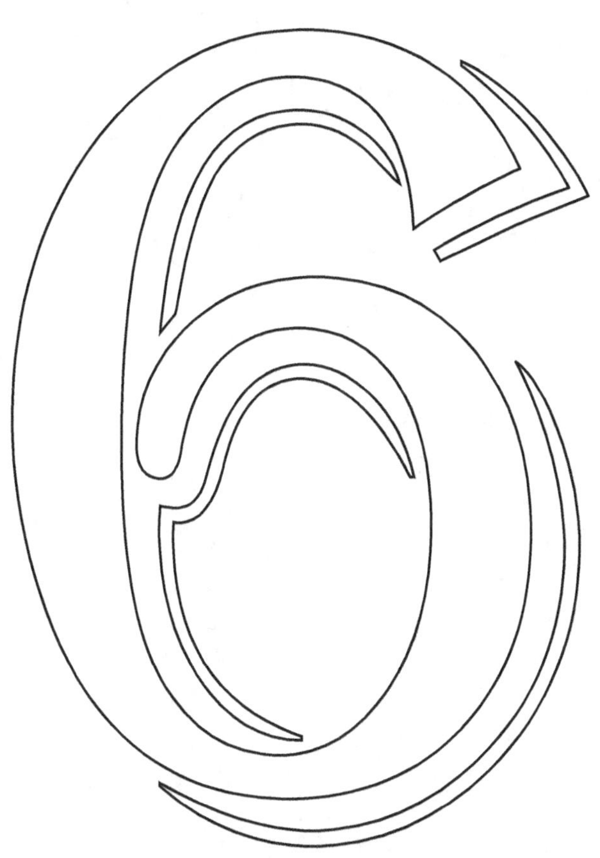

Trace the word THREE

SIX   SIX   SIX

SIX   SIX   SIX

SIX   SIX   SIX

7 Seven

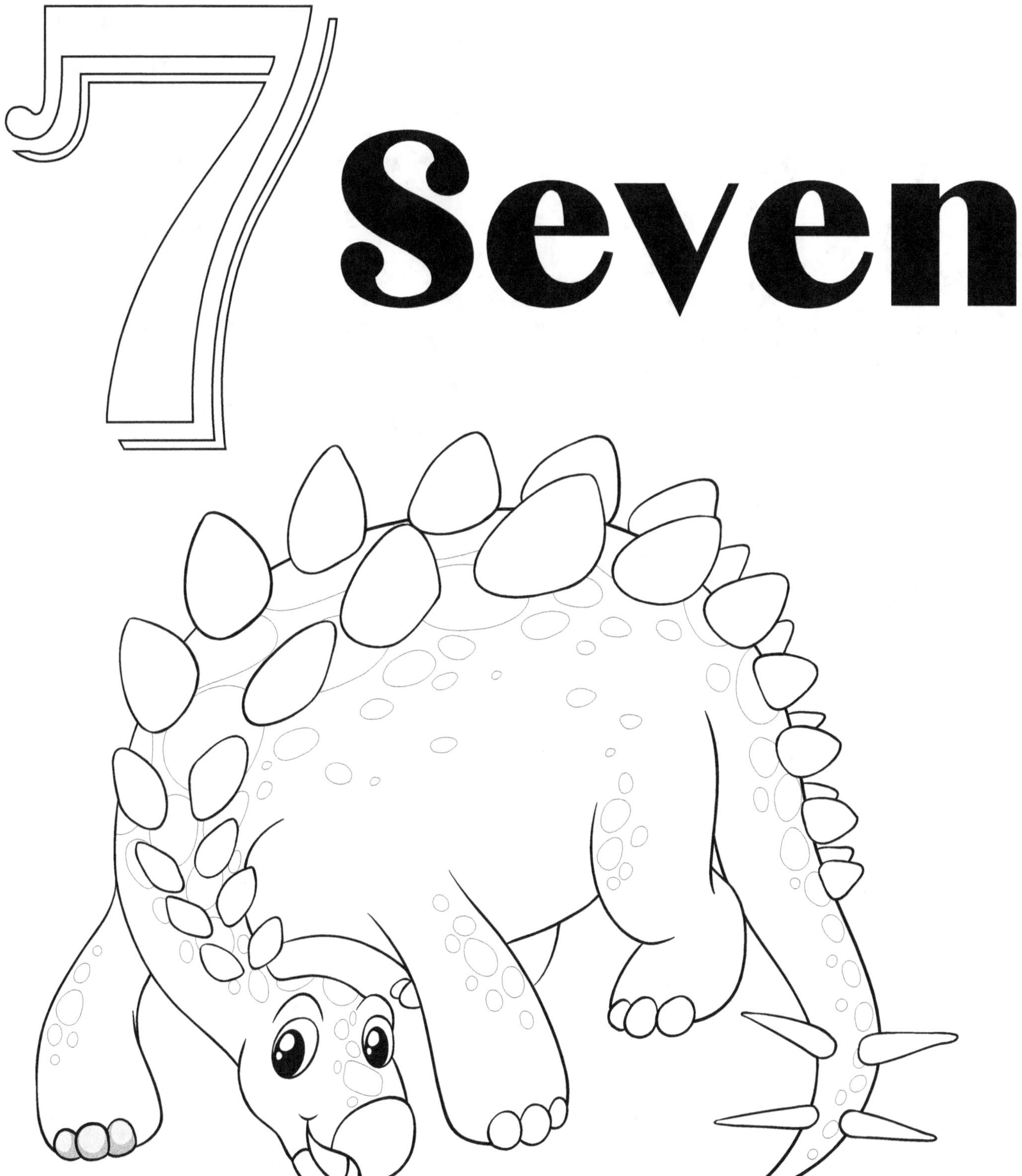

7

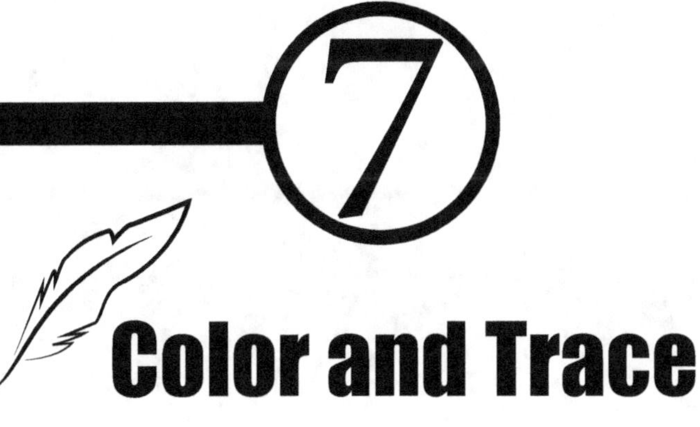

Color and Trace

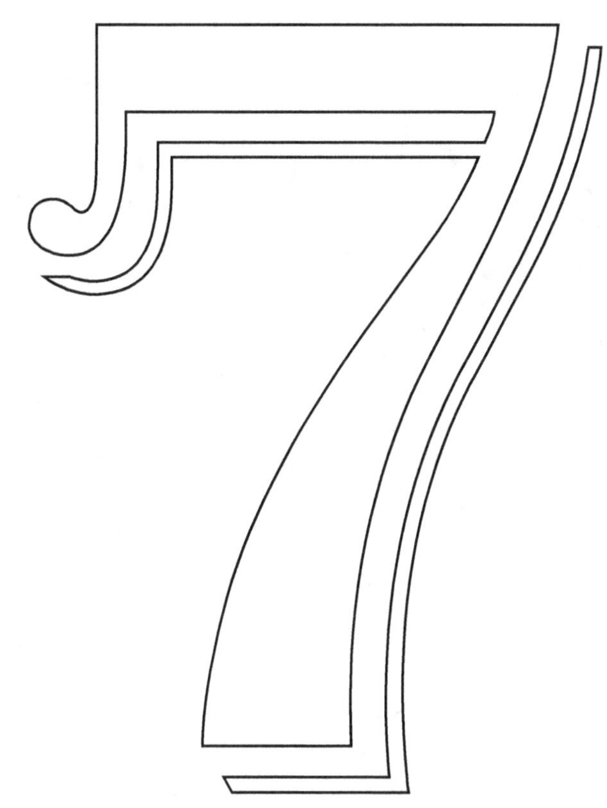

Trace the word SEVEN

SEVEN seven seven

seven seven seven

seven seven seven

8 Eight

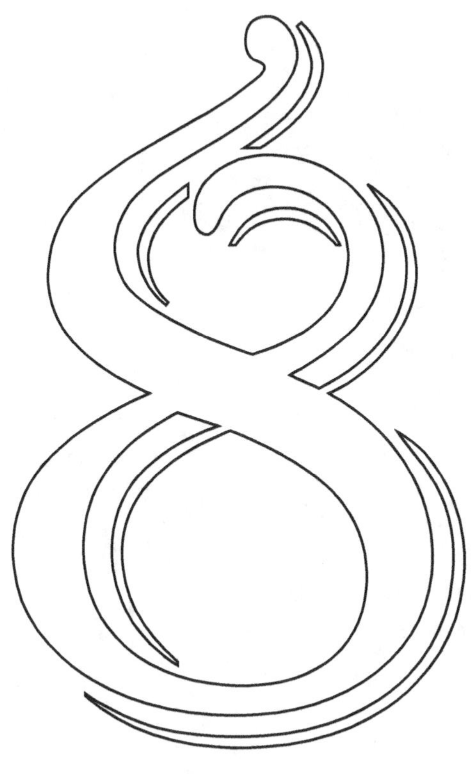

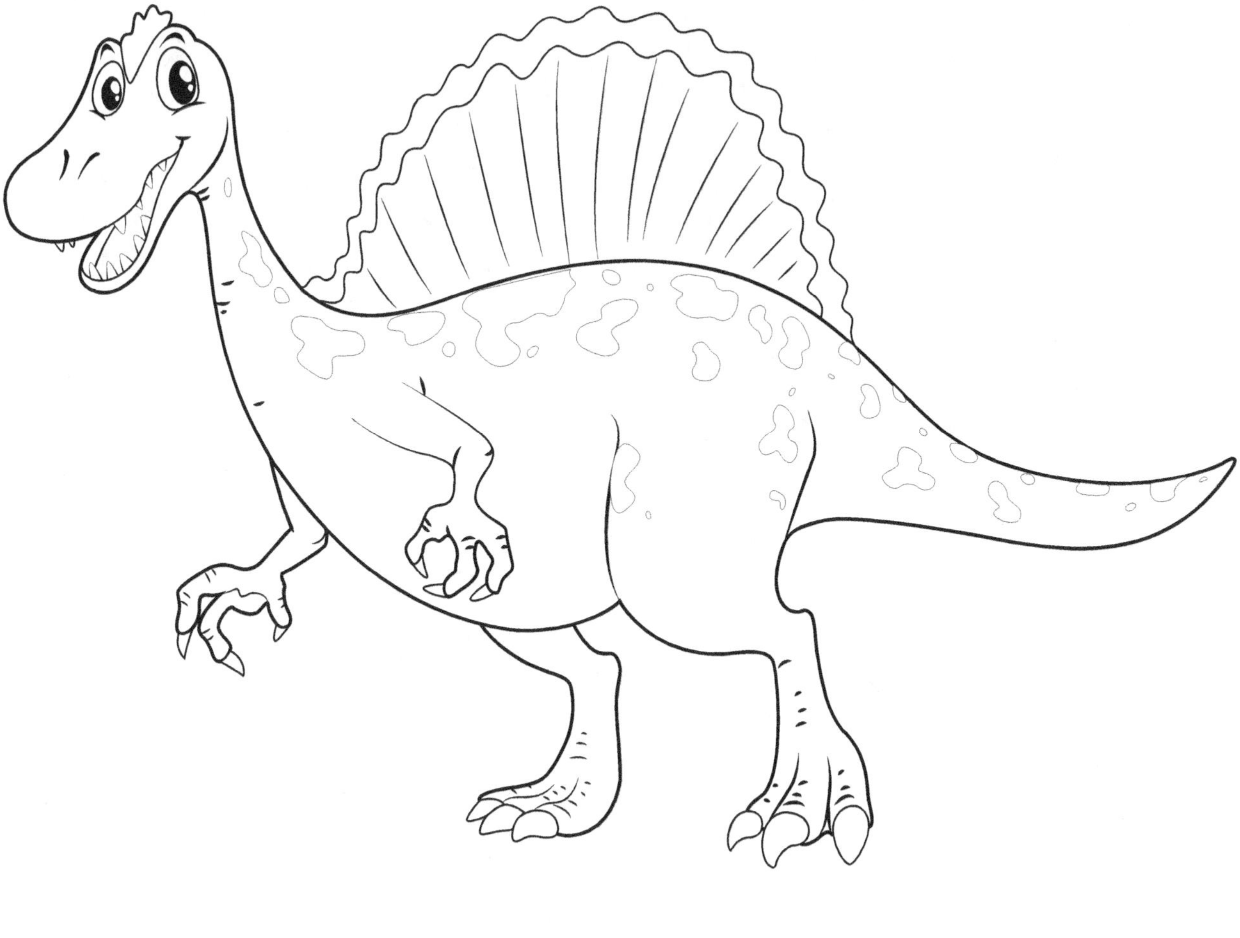

Trace the number

8   8   8   8   8

8   8   8   8   8

8   8   8   8   8

8   8   8   8   8

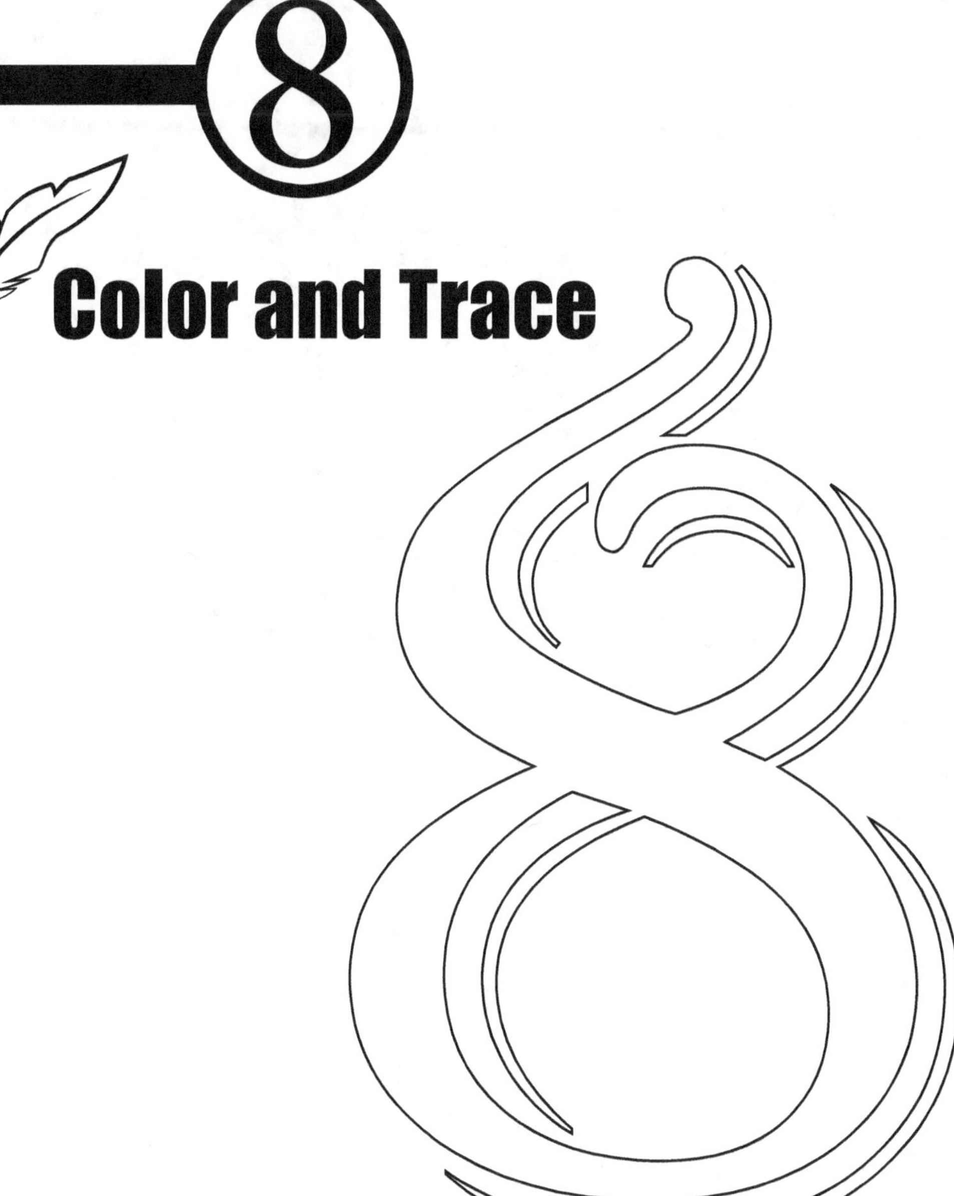

Color and Trace

Trace the word EIGHT

Eight   eight   eight
eight   eight   eight
eight   eight   eight

9 Nine

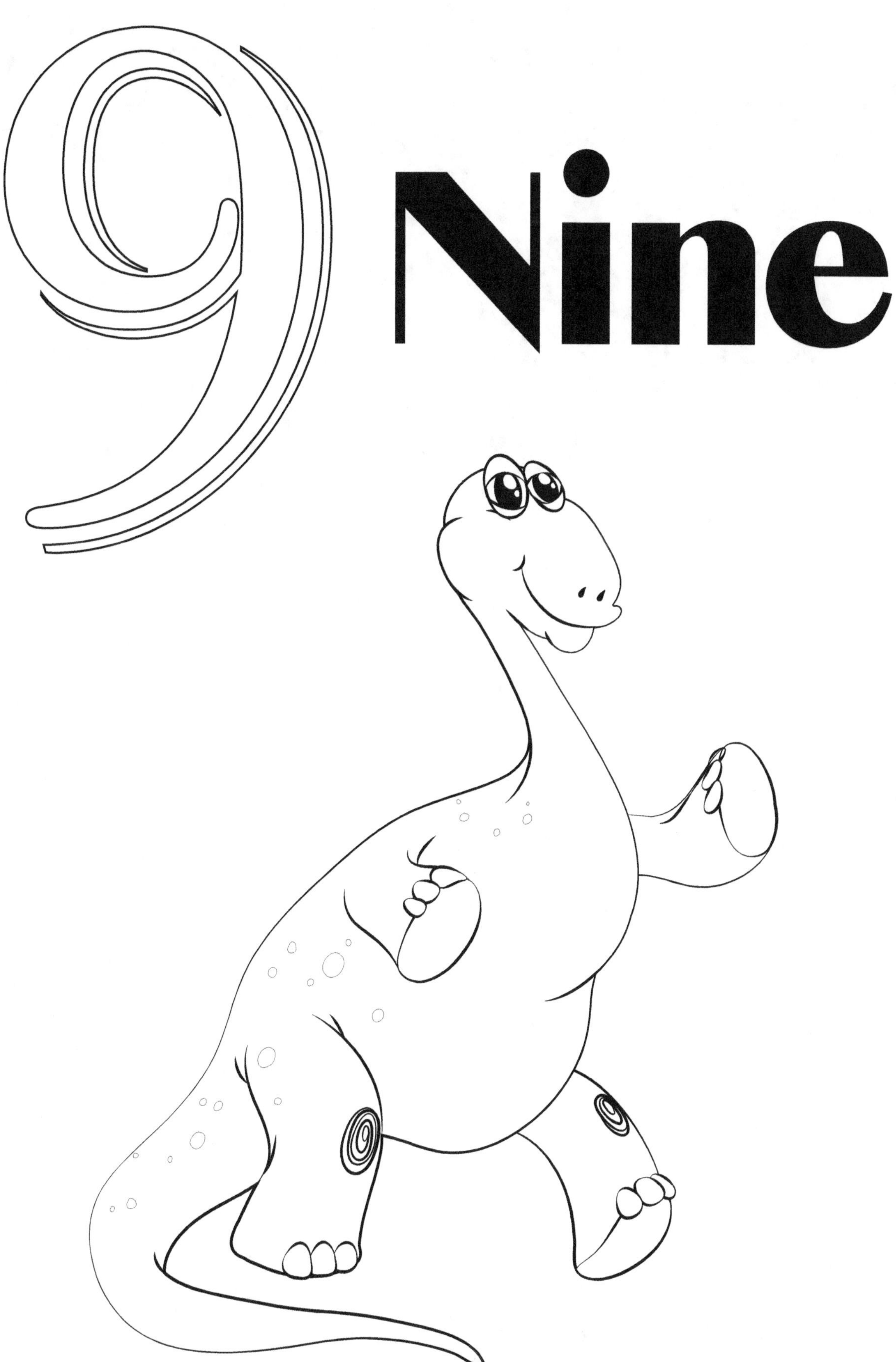

Trace the number

9

Color and Trace

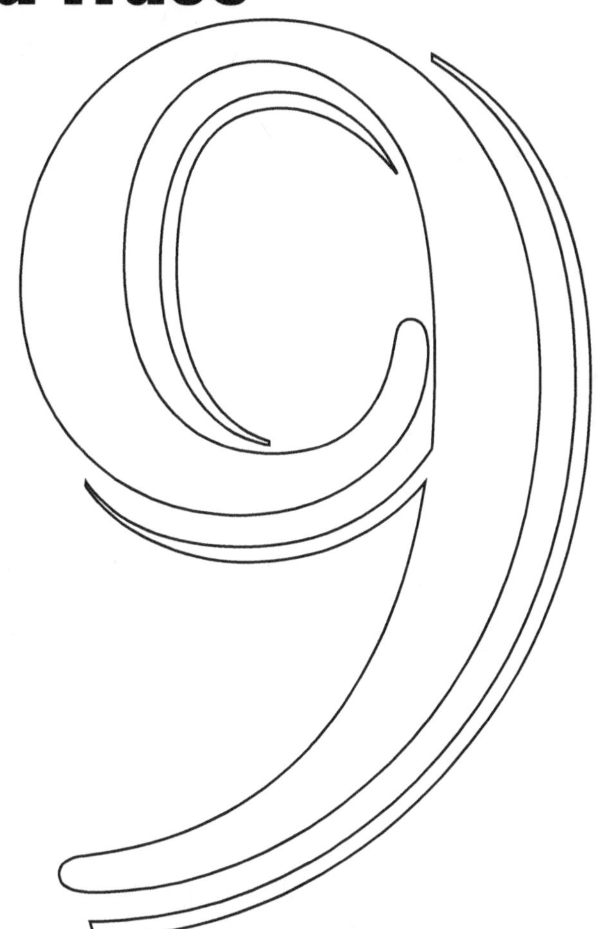

Trace the word NINE

Nine   nine   nine

nine   nine   nine

nine   nine   nine

Your child learn basic math
with many different fun activities